DOG TRAINING

Train Your Dog Positively With Minimal Effort, Maximum Enjoyment

Ronald Clark

© **Copyright 2016 - All rights reserved.**

In no way is it legal to reproduce, duplicate, or transmit any part of this document in either electronic means or in printed format. Recording of this publication is strictly prohibited and any storage of this document is not allowed unless with written permission from the publisher. All rights reserved.

The information provided herein is stated to be truthful and consistent, in that any liability, in terms of inattention or otherwise, by any usage or abuse of any policies, processes, or directions contained within is the solitary and utter responsibility of the recipient reader. Under no circumstances will any legal responsibility or blame be held against the publisher for any reparation, damages, or monetary loss due to the information herein, either directly or indirectly.

Respective authors own all copyrights not held by the publisher.

Legal Notice:
This book is copyright protected. This is only for personal use. You cannot amend, distribute, sell, use, quote or paraphrase any part or the content within this book without the consent of the author or copyright owner. Legal action will be pursued if this is breached.

Disclaimer Notice:
Please note the information contained within this document is for educational and entertainment purposes only. Every attempt has been made to provide accurate, up to date and reliable complete information. No warranties of any kind are expressed or implied. Readers acknowledge that the author is not engaging in the rendering of legal, financial, medical or professional advice.

By reading this document, the reader agrees that under no circumstances are we responsible for any losses, direct or indirect, which are incurred as a result of the use of information contained within this document, including, but not limited to, —errors, omissions, or inaccuracies.

Contents

Introduction 7
What's in a name? 9
The easy way to potty train 11
The definitive crate training guide 15
The most important obedience commands 23
Dealing with the bite 33
How to deal with separation anxiety in dogs 47
Strategies to stop incessant barking 51
Spaying or neutering your dog 55
Dog sitting 65
Adopting dogs 67
Fostering a dog 69
Dogs that eat their own... 81
Closing thoughts 83
Bonus Chapter: Get some love! 85

Introduction

There's a lot of joy involved in bringing a puppy home. Some of you reading this book may have already experienced that feeling. We have their unconditional love, ever-positive attitude, and the constant physical form of attention. There's a whole lot in store for any pet owner. Perhaps what we enjoy most is the fact that dogs may grow old but never grow up!

Unfortunately, not every story has a romantic start. Many a time, pet owners are met with frustration as they are unable to understand how to work with their dog to form an agreement. This could be a scenario where your dog creates a mess, incessantly barks or simply doesn't listen to you. You just aren't able to figure it out.

If you've picked up this book before you've brought your puppy home, good call! The more prepared you are, the better it is for the both of you. If you're reading this after experiencing a little frustration, don't worry! The tips and techniques in this book will help you resolve your anxiety and ensure that you build a positive, rewarding relationship with your dog.

I've written this book with one simple goal - to be as practical a guide as possible. This is your how-to book, and I've written it in a way that ensures you can implement the techniques with ease. By the end of this book, you will be able to:

- Build a positive relationship with your dog
- Potty-train your dog with easy techniques
- Train your dog to respond to simple commands
- Reinforce positive behavior
- Deal with teething and barking issues
- Have fun along the way

Of course, there's a lot more to offer in this book and you can get a snapshot of it from the table of contents. Needless to say, the last point is critical; there is no reason why you can't have a pleasant experience training your dog. As long as you look at things from the right perspective, this can be an enjoyable process.

Remember, your personal goal is to ensure that you and your dog experience positivity throughout and are able to have a truly fulfilling relationship. After all, training does provide your dog with the mental stimulation he or she needs, and it's not just about the 'discipline'.

So go ahead, turn the pages and experience a new world with your pet. After all, the both of you deserve it.

What's in a name?

Apparently, everything! The process of training your dog to do anything is so much easier when he responds to your call.

Needless to say, response to a name can make your job easier. If you ever need to let your dog off the leash, give them some free time or simply let them play in their space, responsiveness allows you to ensure that he comes back.

To start with, you'd want to make sure your dog has a simple name, one that they would easily be able to recognize. A one or two-syllable name is perfect. "Tommy" or "Roger" are some of the common examples. Here are a few ways in which you can ensure you get your dog to identify with his name.

1. **The positive game** – You want to ensure that you only associate positive elements to your dog's name. This is yet another way you can build a positive relationship with your dog. The beauty of most training is there doesn't need to be any negativity. Ensure you are in a quiet place, ideally at home. Call out to your dog with his name when he's a little away from you. If or when he responds and turns around to look at you, flash a big smile with some words of appreciation. If he comes near you, offer him a treat or a toy. At the very least, play with your dog. These are ways in which you can create a positive association with his name.

2. **Play the chase** – A great way to ensure your dog has positive reinforcement is to play a game of chase. This is simple. Call out to your dog and move away so that he chases you. Keep using his name and repeat the process. When your dog catches up to you, you could either play with him or give him a treat. If you don't see your dog chasing you, use a toy as an incentive or nudge him playfully.

3. **Avoid negative terms** – In the training process, you want to avoid any negative terms while using your pup's name. At a later stage, this may be ok. When your pup is still getting used to hearing his name, it's important to stay positive. As far as possible, avoid reprimanding your pup using his name during the training process. Simple commands like "Tommy, Come!" should do the trick. Anything else would work as well.

4. **Test your pup** – This essentially means calling out to your pup as you play fetch or when they're playing with one of their favorite toys. This can help you test their responsiveness. Remember to add something positive to the mix if you're taking them away from something they enjoy doing.

5. **Keep it alive** – You don't just want this to be about positive reinforcements. Keep using your pup's name all the time. Don't confuse him with nicknames. When you're feeding him, playing with him, or at times just connecting, go ahead and call him by name. Show him some love, but gradually, you can tone that down.

6. **Don't expect perfection** – It's possible that your dog may respond to his name all the time, but that's not always the case. As long as your dog responds often enough, you can pat yourself on the back. You're not going to get your dog to dance to your tune anytime you want him to! Have patience in the process. Not all breeds respond in a quick manner and you may notice different learning curves.

The easy way to potty train

This is the second chapter for a reason. Every pet owner wants to figure this out. How do we potty-train our dogs? Well, there's obviously a clear method here, but before we get to train your new family member, we need to train you first!

- **Be patient** - A puppy is often never completely potty-trained until they turn about six months old. Now that may sound like a long time to you, but understand that this is akin to having a newborn in your house. They simply don't have control over their bowel movements and they're yet to 'find a spot'. Often, puppies aren't going to be easy to train for the first three months, but they show clear progress after that period as they learn better and have more control. With an older dog, this could be an easier process. With puppies, it's a different ballgame.

- **Be around** - You must understand that it is important you or someone you trust is with your puppy as much as possible. Not only does he need your love and attention to build a positive relationship, he also needs your help in potty-training for the first few months. The more you're around, the easier it is to make the learning process quicker. Of course, there are some things you can do to train your dog when you aren't around, but that doesn't help the overall goal.

- **Stay positive** - Pet owners often get frustrated when their pets soil areas they aren't supposed to. It's important to understand that negativity towards your pet only causes fear and doesn't really get the job done. Positive reinforcements are needed when they do the right things. That includes your mood too!

Now that we have *you* out of the way, let's get to your little one. For the first two to three months, you are going to experience some difficulty and you'll have to work with it. Here's what you need to do:

- **Choose the spot** - Stating the obvious, but it's important that you choose the spot. It's shouldn't be a very large area. Remember, dogs work with scent. So decide where you want to see the litter go!

- **Meal time** - You need to ensure that you feed your pup at regular timings. Besides the obvious health benefits, this allows you to predict his behavior and train him in a better fashion. Pups have a digestive tract that works quite quickly, so this can be quite helpful. Keeping a regular feeding schedule simply makes the job easier.

- **How pups poop** - That may have not sounded right but it's still important to know. Remember, a pup's digestive system work differently from that of an adult dog. Pups tend to eliminate five to thirty minutes after consumption of any item. The size of your dog itself is an indicator in itself. Smaller dogs tend to defecate more often as their metabolic rate is higher. Ensure you take them to the designated spot within that time range.

- **Positive reinforcement** - It's no secret that dogs love treats. The best way to ensure they go to their designated spot is to give them a treat immediately after they eliminate. This is how they learn to go to the right place.

- **Avoid negative reinforcement** - You're going to see your puppy make mistakes along the way, and that can happen quite often. That's fine and it's part of the learning process. Remember, without bowel control it becomes quite difficult for your pup to keep it all in! Stay patient and avoid reprimanding him. Fear often does a pup no good and only has him repeat the behavior when you aren't looking. Yes, some dogs are sly that way. Focus on the positive reinforcements when they do use their designated spot.

- **Clean the scent** - If your pup does eliminate in any other spot, make sure you clean the area to get rid of the scent. If it's in the house, use cleaning liquid and scrub it away. This ensures that your pup does not relate to that spot again.

- **Moving the act** - What do you do if you catch your pup in the act? Well, it's simple enough. If he is urinating, lift him immediately and move him to the designated area. Doing this when your pup is defecating could be a bad idea though; you don't really want to create a mess and your pup may not immediately stop. In such a scenario, let it be and clean the area once they are done.

As you can see, the process of potty-training your dog is actually simple but requires you to be vigilant and do your bit. Without your constant involvement, your pup's learning curve is going to be slow and you don't want to miss the ball.

Working with an adult dog

Some of you may have done the noble thing and taken in an abandoned or rescued dog. These dogs may have not been house trained depending on their growing conditions. The good news is that the process stays the same. If anything, you might be able to space out your walks given that their digestive tract now works differently. Adult dogs take between four to six bathroom breaks a day. The best way to space it out is to take your dog for the walk first thing in the morning, thrice in the day, and twice after dinner. You'll figure out the schedule yourself.

What to watch out for

Even after doing all the right things, you may still notice that your dog hasn't consistently picked up on the habit. There could be several reasons for this:

- **Dietary changes** - If you happened to change what you feed your dog, there could be a change in his bowel movements too. In these cases, you may notice loose stools, diarrhea and other common symptoms. If he shows no signs of improvement, make the journey to the vet.

- **Medical issues** - There are many medical issues that can cause irregular stool release. This could be related to diabetes, neurological disorders and many other such issues. You can rule this out with regular vet checkups. If you do notice such issues, take it forward with the qualified practitioners.

- **Gastric trouble** - Just like humans, dogs can face gastric trouble too. You may notice a pattern change, and of course, in the stool as well. There are several medicines that can be prescribed to sort this out for your dog.

In all of these cases, the vet is your best friend too. There are other possible concerns, such as dogs that suffer from anxiety or stress. A lot of that can be handled through what we cover in this book and may just be a function of spending time with your dog. If that doesn't resolve it, get professional help.

If you've already been reading a little bit about dog training, you may have noticed that we have not yet covered another way to train your dog or puppy when it comes to dealing with his potty. We have an entire chapter dedicated to that important subject - the art of crate training.

The definitive crate training guide

A lot of folks believe that crate training is inhumane and cruel. It is imagined to be a place where you 'confine' a pet to. Nothing could be further from the truth. The reality is *how* you train your dog with respect to the crate. In fact, dogs can experience the *opposite* of what many people imagine.

With the right training, your dog will treat the crate as an area of comfort and security. It can almost become his own little space. A home within a home, if you will! Even then, some people are uncomfortable with the idea and that's fine. Many dogs are trained well-enough without the use of a crate. It still remains one of the best ways to train your dogs and if you still believe that this is 'wrong', let me assure you that this chapter will help you set those worries aside.

Before we get to that, let's be sure that you're up to speed on this.

What really is crate training?

Simply put, it's an effective way to ensure that your puppy is well-trained. You would 'confine' (I cringe in using that word because that's not the experience your pup would go through) your pup to a 'crate' of sorts, or a small area. This is to ensure they treat this crate as their 'den', and dogs do not like to defecate in their den. As long as your pup is handled at the right time, he can be trained quickly to defecate at the right spots.

This is a temporary arrangement and *not* meant to be a long-term plan. The purpose of the crate is to help the training process. I cannot emphasize that enough. This is also very useful when you aren't at home. Once he gets used to the crate, it's an easier situation to manage if you happen to step out. Do not confuse that for the reason they are in a crate! It is an additional benefit, but crate training is meant to be for times you are around and purely for the purpose of potty-training.

Remember, crate training is not just to help you; it can also be very beneficial for your dog. Wouldn't you keep your child in a crib or a playpen at times? The treatment does not have to be any different.

Why you should consider crate training

- **Bladder and bowel control** - We looked at this concept in detail in the previous chapter. A crate can be critical in helping a puppy have better control over their system. This is because dogs don't like soiling their own den and will quicken their learning process. Of course, you can't restrict them to the crate purely based on that! We'll get to the right method a little later.
- **Den instinct** - All dogs have a natural den instinct, an area they adopt as 'theirs'. The crate can very well become their den, and their relationship towards it will be similar to how one would treat a home. This instinct can be created through positivity and does not have to be forced upon your dog.

- **Damage control** - The crate can help your dog stay out of any trouble. You can't always be around to watch over your dog. You might have to head to work or simply get a good night's sleep! The crate can ensure that your dog stays voluntarily under control.

- **Behavior control** - Sometimes our dogs just need to learn to relax! Puppies and dogs tend to be excitable and often enough, it's not just you who needs a break. Crate training ensures that they stay calm when required and helps them get a little down-time.

- **Safety** - When you are in your car, a safe spot for your dog happens to be the crate. I know, your dog would rather have the wind blow in their face! You can make the call, but it's still important information to have in a long-haul journey. The comfort of your dog in a crate helps when safety is paramount.

Convinced? Well, all these benefits only count if you train your dog right. How comfortable he feels in a crate is *your* responsibility. You don't have to crate your dog for the long-term. As long as they reach a voluntary stage with the usage, there's no need to enforce anything as long as they are sufficiently trained. The first step, of course, is ensuring that your dog gets the right den.

Choosing the right crate

The first question to answer is how big the crate should be. Well, you may want it to be comfortable enough for your pup. Don't get carried away! You're using the crate for a few months and for the purpose of potty-training, so you can't have to it too big. It needs to be big enough for him to move around, but not for him to defecate in. In a large crate, your pup may very well be comfortable choosing a corner to let loose. It needs to be just big enough for him to turn around in, sleep and stand up.

There are many types of crates, but we're going with the two most common ones.

Wire crates – Wire crates are great for storage purposes as some are easily foldable. It's also helpful for dogs that happen to live in a hot climate. Many of these crates have a removable floor tray that can be cleaned as and when required. It's also worth mentioning that some of these crates have separators if you want to control the space your pup has within the crate.

The issues you may face is for the purpose of transportation, since these crates aren't exactly light. It can also be a little noisy when you move it around. If you're one for aesthetics, let's just say that wire crates don't really add to the décor.

Plastic crates – Plastic crates are great for transportation even if you're catching a flight. There are also times when certain adventurous pups are known to be able to get out of wired crates. Plastic crates don't really provide for that option.

The downside is that the visibility is low and your pup might get frustrated if he isn't able to see much. These crates are also harder to clean, especially if your pup falls sick.

There are many other variations, but these are the two most common ones. Ultimately choose what you think is wise for you and your pup. Whichever crate you choose, the size element we discussed is important to ensure that the training is effective.

The crate training guide

Now that you have your crate, it's time to figure out how you can get the job done. Here's a step-by-step guide to help you through the process.

1. **Prepare the crate** – If you want your pup to take to the crate, you ought to make it attractive! We don't really mean decorating it as such, but there are a few things you could do. Start with placing a soft, easy blanket in the crate. You can also add a few chew toys for your pup to play with. Your job is to ensure that your pup enjoys his time in the crate. Preparing the area can make the process easier.

2. **Crate introduction** – The biggest mistake you can make is to force your dog in to the crate. You want your pup to be able to do this voluntarily. In some cases, this could take several days. It really depends on the comfort level of your dog. Ensure that you introduce your pup to the crate in a fun manner and encourage him to explore the crate. The toys inside help. Your tone of voice can be more critical to achieving this than you think. Try sounding as

pleasant as possible.

Sometimes toys alone may not cut it. Food treats could do the trick. If your dog is still not moving in, place some small treats inside the area. If he or she still isn't entering the crate, just be patient. Place the treats in different areas within the crate and experiment with it.

By now you should be fine. If after several days you still notice some resistance, try a set of different toys or treats. Usually, you won't have to work this hard. Your dog should take to the crate sooner than you think, but one always faces exceptions!

3. **Feeding time** – In the beginning your dog is possibly just curious and gets in the crate, but that's not your goal. You want them to feel comfortable in that small area. They say that the way to a man's heart is through his stomach. Thankfully for you, that rule extends to dogs as well!

   Feeding your dog near the crate can ensure that he or she will have more positive associations with it. Some dogs may enter the crate without much effort on your part. For other dogs, you may need to ease them in. Start with placing the food near the entry point and then slowly all the way in the crate. Once your notice your dog start to get comfortable inside, close the crate.

   This step has to be done right though. Initially, you should open the crate when they're done eating. Every time you feed your pup, leave the crate closed a little longer. You should ideally get him comfortable with being in the crate for five or ten minute durations.

4. **Handling any trouble** – It's in this process that you may notice different reactions. Learn to understand and listen to your dog. These are the

moments where you can learn to build a positive relationship with your pup.

If your dog begins to whimper of whine, he's obviously not as comfortable. You may need to space out the time you keep him in the crate. You may also need to show him some tough love! Ignore the whining and see if it stops. You don't want to encourage a manipulation tactic, do you? Be smart about this, of course. You're the best judge at that point of time.

5. **Time in The crate** – Once your pup gets comfortable in the crate in that five to ten minute range, you can start extending their time in there. This part has to be done a little carefully, but can be quite simple if you just follow the instructions laid out here.
    a. You want your pup to get used to the crate even if it isn't meal time. Call him or her over in a friendly tone and offer a treat when your pup enters the crate. You could even use a toy as incentive. Make sure to include some praise and be expressive!
    b. If you want to train your pup with a command, this would be a good time. Associate a command with asking your pup to enter the crate. We'll be speaking more of these methods in later chapters.
    c. Once your pup is in the crate, stay around for some time. Your goal is to reach a point when you can leave. So if he is fine, you should leave for about five or ten minutes. You can come back and then check on him.
    d. As long as he is fine, don't open the crate yet! Hang around for a while before opening the crate.
    e. Repeat the process and keep increasing the time. When your pup is able to stay in the crate for about thirty to forty-five minutes without

your presence, you've hit a milestone!

6. **The big night** – You can now test and check if your pup is able to spend a night in the crate. Keep the crate nearby so you are within earshot if there's any trouble. When they want to defecate, you're going to hear him wail! You'll want to be able take him to the spot when it's time. Keep in mind that you shouldn't keep your pup in the crate for more than four to five hours at a stretch. In fact, they shouldn't even be in the crate that long before five months of age.

7. **Letting go** – Did that sound too dramatic for you? What I really mean is you can now see whether you can actually leave the house while your pup is in the crate. Remember, the goal is not for you to put your pup in the crate for the sake of it and just leave him there. This is for you to be able to potty-train your pup without your presence. Leave in a very normal manner and be back within a few hours. No emotional goodbyes! You want your pup looking at this with absolutely normalcy. Similarly, keep your arrivals low-key and normal. Don't be very excited.

Let me say this again; you must never crate your dog for more than four to five hours at a time. A thumb rule is the time a pup can be in a crate depends on how old he is. That essentially means add an hour for every month. You can stop crating your pup once you feel they are sufficiently trained. At times, dogs take to their crates so that's obviously fine. If you're going to leave your dog in a crate for four to five hours, ensure that there is sufficient water available within reach.

Crating adult dogs

As we've discussed earlier, it's possible that you have adopted a dog that hasn't been potty-trained. If possible, it's important you understand your dog's history. Has he been mistreated and has already been unnecessarily confined to a space for long hours? You'll need to be sensitive to your dog's needs and background.

There's good news and not-so-good news here. The good news is that your dog already has bowel control, so you can space out the walks. The not-so-good news is that you'll probably experience some resistance to crate training. Remember, a pup's mind is fresh but an adult dog needs to unlearn old habits.

The method stays exactly the same. You'll just have to be a lot more patient and ensure your dog doesn't have a background that could affect him psychologically. Even then, it's simply a matter of time if you think crate training is a necessity for your dog.

The most important obedience commands

It's now time to send your dog to obedience school. You do ultimately want your dog to listen to you and work with you in your relationship. For that very purpose, commands become quite important in the training process. Just learning some commands can help tacking any behavioral issues that could crop up. For that simple reason, you should ensure that your dog plays a listening role with you.

I've done my best to order this in the right way. By that I mean when you train your dog with new commands, you can use the old ones to help you along with it. For example, your dog's only going to find it easier to shake your hand if he's sitting in the first place!

With that in mind, here are some commands for you to work with:

1. **Sit**
   This seems like the obvious first one, doesn't it? Teaching your dog to sit is just about what everyone wants. The good news is that this is fairly simple, and with a few repetitive actions, you should be good to go.

   a. You'll want to use a treat for this. Hold a treat close to your dog, but don't feed him just yet!
   b. As your dog gets a whiff of the treat, move your hand up and his head will begin to follow you. Essentially, his bottom will reach near the floor.
   c. This is your shot! As he nears the sitting position, command your dog to "sit". Once he does so, give him what he deserves. You need to be enthusiastic too. Let your dog feel the love!

   You're essentially associating the movement to the command, and over time, your dog will understand the meaning of the word. Repeat this a few times and you'll begin to see the difference. Once you feel that this is occurring consistently, practice the command without the treat in the day-to-day scenario.

2. **Stay**

   Now that you've taught your dog to sit, the next step is seeing if you can get your dog to practice restraint and be patient. Having your dog 'stay' in the seated position is one such way of doing that. This process is a little less simple, but still fairly easy to implement.

   a. Once you get your dog to sit, tell him to 'stay' and place your hand on his back, without any pressure.
   b. Slowly walk around your dog. At this point, he may get up. Gently press his rump down and repeat the 'stay' command, so he understands that he needs to stay seated.
   c. Reach a point where you can make a complete circle around your dog with him in the 'stay' position.
   d. Repeat the entire process, but now, see if you can do so without having to place your hand on your dog.
   e. At the end of the process, give him a treat or show him some affection. The positive reinforcement helps in all forms of training.

   During the entire process, make sure you're not moving too fast. Feel free to experiment. You can start moving in different directions, ask your dog to stay in the position in a different environment and so on. You eventually want to reach a point where you can get your dog to 'stay' for a full minute. Needless to say, you'll need to ease him into it. Start with five second intervals and gradually increase the duration.

   This could take longer than you imagine. In most cases, you're asking a high-energy pup to stay in one place. Give it time and he'll come around.

3. **The Yes and No**

   We all want to be able to tell our dog when they're doing something right and when they're not. Over time, they'll get the gist of what you expect and how they can keep their behavior intact. You can train your dog to understand this even as you train him to do other things. This ensures they know when they've done something right.

Your tone and excitement (or lack of it) is everything! As you're training your dog, say "Yes!" in an enthusiastic tone when they perform a task correctly. You can go ahead and show a little bit of physical affection too. For example, when your dog gets in the crate on your command, you could say "Yes!" flashing a big smile.

You can use "No" when your dog does something inappropriate. You may not want to use this not as much in training but also in situations around the house. If you catch your dog in midst of an unfavorable act, Say "Noo!" with a loud and serious tone. Ensure that your face matches your voice, of course! What you may then want to do is practice moving that negative statement to positive and direct your dog to do something else. For example, if your dog happens to create a mess, say "Nooo" in a firm tone and redirect your dog.

In both these situations, it's important that you catch your dog in the act, and use those words *right at the moment*. The immediacy can ensure that you dog is able to associate the words with the act.

4. **The Give and the Get**
   These commands can take a little while for your dog to respond to and you have to keep your eye out for different behavioral traits. We'll come to that a bit later, but let's first understand how the training process works here. The good news is that you can even play with your dog for him to learn these commands.

a. **Give** – If your dog is holding on to something, simply place your hand on the item and say "Give" in a stern voice. Stern does not necessarily mean negative. It's just important that you sound clear and in control. If your dog immediately releases the item, great! Let's face it though, that probably won't happen as much right off the cuff. Keep repeating this action till he does let go. Once he releases the item, immediately display positivity. This is a good time for your enthusiastic "Yes!" to make an entrance.

Some dogs may still be quite stubborn and not let go. You'll need to be patient with him. Avoid tugging at the item as many dogs look at that action as playtime and simply won't let go. The ideal way is to place your finger on the side of their mouth or in their gum and repeat the "Give" command. Apply a little pressure, but nothing hurtful. Slowly, your pup will let go as he won't be too comfortable! Once he lets go, go for the resounding "Yes!" and give him some love. You could give your pup a treat.

b. **Get** – You could use one of two commands – "Get" or "Get it" as the case may be. This part of the training could be fun. You could train your dog with a simple game of fetch and then test it in regular situations. All you have to do is pick an item, any item. It doesn't necessarily have to be a favorite toy. A ball is a good pick.

First, catch your dog's attention with the item. A bit of a tease, if you will! Hold it a little near your dog. Then throw the item about ten feet away from you, and ask your dog to "Get it!"

In most cases his natural instinct is going to be to run towards the item. Continue with the command. With his curiosity, he'll want to pick it up. Your timing here is important! At the exact time you see him pick it up, encourage him. You could say "Get it! Yes!" and then get the attention of your dog back (you could call him by his name) to you and ask him to "Give" it to you. Once he does that, shower him with praise.

This may require a bit of repetition with simple commands. Soon after, you can check if your dog responds to the command without you having to throw an item. Keep repeating the process and you've got yourself a getting and giving dog!

5. **Leave it!**

   This command is useful when you want your dog to let go of an item or is tugging at something he isn't supposed to. Here's how you can ensure he leaves an item when needed.

   a. Hold a treat between your thumb and index finger. Show him the treat with your palm facing upwards. It needs to be in his visibility.
   b. He's going to try prying it loose. Say "Leave it" and close your first. Your dog is probably going to look at you with a quizzical expression and that's fine.
   c. Any behavior that exists to manipulate you, ignore it! He's probably going to try barking or may look at you longingly.
   d. The minute his attention moves away from the hand, say "Yes!' in a cheerful tone and give him a treat.
   e. Keep repeating the process.
   f. Test the command without you having to close your hand.
   g. Do this in different situations and environments to see if works across situations. You could try this outdoors.

6. **Jump away**

   You may want your dog to respond to jump commands as well. This is useful for several reasons. For example, if you find your dog on something they shouldn't be on, you can have them get off. If you want him to give you a bit of a snuggle, you can even command him to jump on you! Of course, you'll have the words to help you free yourself from that hug too.

   a. Ensure you have a steady surface of sorts where you can practice with your dog. A metal or a wooden box of sorts should do the trick. Any flat surface that isn't very high for him should work fine.
   b. Walk your dog towards the box and tap the top of it with the command "Jump on!" You can use his name, of course. Do this a few times and see if he responds.
   c. If he doesn't respond to the general instruction, use a treat as incentive on the box, with you holding it. Ensure you use the words "Jump on!" as he makes it to the treat. You want the command to be heard.
   d. Once he does jump on, give him the treat of course. If he did it without the treat, give him the encouraging yes and display positivity.
   e. Let him stay on for a few minutes. If he tries to get off a little early, command him to 'stay'. You want him to get off the box only when you give the go-ahead.
   f. Once a few minutes pass, command him to "Jump Off". Motion your hand to where you want him to jump to. Do this a few times. It's important you have a joyous tone. It needs to be a game for him.
   g. Once he gets off, you can go ahead and show some encouragement.

7. **Down, boy!**

   You've already taught your dog to 'stay'. Now you may want your dog to park at a particular spot for a longer period of time. For that, you need him to be able to not just stay but to rest as well. The training is very similar to how you taught him to sit, so here are the steps:

a. Hold the doggie treat in front of his nose like you did during the training where you had him sit.
b. Instead of moving it up this time, slowly move the treat to the ground. As soon as your dog moves down, state the 'down' command to create the association.
c. Repeat the steps again so that the verbal cue is reinforced and your dog registers the command. The principle is the same.
d. As with everything else, shower your dog with praise when he does lock down and give him the treat.
e. If you still face trouble with your dog going down, work with a different treat or simply have patience through it. As always, every dog works with different learning curves. I cannot stress that enough.
f. Take short breaks as needed before you repeat the process. You want to combine this with the stay command as you move away.

8. **Go to bed**

    This could very well be the crate too and you can always have multiple beds. The method can be useful when you need a breather, or you have a guest at home. Another useful time to do this is during your meals so that your dog realizes he must stay calm at these times.

    Having your dog move to his bed is not about punishment. As usual, it needs to have a positive association for him to willingly go when asked to. It doesn't necessarily need to be a bed. You could command your dog to go to his place or spot.

    a. Get your dog's bed ready and comfortable. Your

dog needs to enjoy going there. Just as we discussed making the crate attractive, the same rules apply here.
b. You want to direct your dog close to the spot, so he's nearby when you need him trained. Start sweeping your hand and point to the location along with the command. You can choose the word. This could be "bed", "go to bed", "spot" or anything else you'd like to call it.
c. If your dog doesn't move there directly, use the treat to lure him to the spot.
d. Once he finds himself on the spot, shower him with praise and give him the treat. Mark the behavior with a resounding "Yes" and display the same enthusiasm we keep speaking of.
e. You now want him to settle on the bed. This is when the "down" command that we just covered comes in handy. Give the command as soon as he gets on the bed or the spot.
f. You want to ensure that your dog learns to spend a duration of time on his bed. You can combine this with the stay command. Another method is to hold the treat away a little longer from your dog, and increase the duration each time.
g. You can now try this from a different room. Give the command of going to bed and see how your dog responds. You can move the bed to another location, so he understands that the spot is on the bed and not a particular spot in one room.
h. If you want to make the tests harder, introduce some distractions. Give him his toy and then instruct him to go to bed to understand how this could work. At this point you could combine commands by asking him to let go to of the toy and follow your instructions.

Dogs do tend to catch on to their spot fast, so you shouldn't face a problem. He should be able to latch on and understand his designated area, just like he did with the crate training process.

Great. You now have some solid commands to work with, and they're all important in their own way. With these set of commands, it simply becomes so much easier to work with your dog.

We're going to now spend the next few chapters looking at how you can deal with certain issues you may come across with your growing dog.

Dealing with the bite

Every pup goes through a teething phase. This is fairly common amongst most animals. We first need to understand that this is completely normal and nothing to be alarmed about. If anything, it's an important phase and one should be concerned if a pup does not go through with this.

You'll begin to notice your pup sinking their teeth into anything. Be it their chew toy or even parts of you! Most of the time it will just be a nip. Needless to say, there are times when it can feel like a lot more than that and could hurt you. There are also rare circumstances where your dog might be trying to assert his dominance over you. That requires a different sort of intervention where the recognition of alpha needs to be clear.

What we're trying to do is help your puppy learn to regulate his bite and have a soft bite that doesn't hurt you. In the training world, we term this as *bite inhibition*. The reason for this training is your pup doesn't understand the sensitivity of your skin and you need to help with that process. This helps everyone around you, including visitors, to be able to play with your pup freely.

To deal with the most common issues, we first need to make sure we avoid the errors that people tend to make.

Mistakes

- **Heavy physical play** – You want to avoid a situation where you are involved in physical activities. This could include playing a game of chase, or just physically engaging with your pup in any manner. Have you ever seen dogs playing with each other? To those uninitiated, it almost looks like a playful wrestle. What you'll also notice is how they use their mouths and tend to nip each other as well. You'll end up encouraging such behavior if you're trying to regulate the bite at that point of time.

- **Physical control** – If your puppy gives you a bit of a bite in a sensitive area, never slap or hit your puppy. Ever. Besides the fact that you might earn my wrath if I find out, it doesn't work. You'll only instigate fear and have a pup that is afraid of you. These may lead to other behavioral issues and you don't want that.

- **Expecting self-realization** – No, your pup will most likely not figure it out on their own and you don't want to start the process when it's too late. You see, stray dogs figure this out as they play with each other and get 'trained'. That may not be the case with your pup. For him to learn bite inhibition, he needs you.

As long as you avoid those situations, you're okay. Helping your pup understand bite inhibition can be easier than you think. So let's get started, shall we?

Proven techniques

- **The yelp**

    The most popular technique, and this also allows you to play with your dog to eventually teach him the 'soft bite'. As we had just discussed, pups usually learn *how* to bite without really hurting the other one when they play with each other. You're replicating this very process with your pup. When you're playing with your dog or generally with them and they start biting your hand, let out a loud 'Ouch' or 'Yelp' when a particular bite is too hurtful. Startle your dog with that exclamation and stop playing with him or move away. Your pup will begin to understand that he shouldn't bite too hard if he wants to be able to play with you.

Over time, you would want your pup to stop biting altogether. You repeat the process of Yelps for bites that may not be as hard so they eventually understand that biting skin is a no-no. It's important that friends and family members are aware of the training process. You don't want them giving mixed signals to your dog and encouraging the biting!

- **Redirection**

    The Yelp technique is great when you are comfortable with your pup and the teething process. Once he crosses six months in age, you shouldn't be seeing the behavior as much. The Redirection technique is what you use when you want your pup to stop biting skin altogether.

    When he bites you, give out a "no!" and provide him with a chewy toy instead. You can also immediately move away and play a game that does not involve physical contact. If you notice any aggression along the way, you need to learn to command your dog to let go of items through the training process described in earlier chapters.

- **Unpleasant associations**

    An unpleasant smell can throw your pup away from biting habits. You could put on a glove that is pasted with an item that you dog doesn't like. They'll understand not to bite it when they dig in over time. Of course, if you've got a smart puppy, they'll figure out the trick. Either way, you will still have the other techniques to work with.

- **Stop feet biting**

    Some pups like to nip at your feet or ankles. An easy way to deal with this is carry a favorite toy of his and distract him with it when it happens. Don't jerk your feet as much, your pup may think you're playing with him. Once he stops taking a nip, shower him with praise and give him the toy. You can also try the yelp technique and see if it works in this situation too.

- **Water spray**

    It's exactly what you think it is. If your pup begins biting, you can spray him lightly with water to dissuade him. This is useful if the other techniques don't work, and it's again about getting your pup to stop biting altogether.

It's important that in the training process you maintain consistency. If you notice very aggressive behavior, I recommend getting a professional to work with your pup as there may be underlying reasons for which you may require an expert.

It's not common to need one, though. Enjoy the nips while it lasts!

How to get your dog friendly with other dogs

Dogs normally get along well with other dogs. I'm sure some of you have had an issue with your furry friend snarling or growling at another dog. Now, this could be an issue for some of us, especially if you want to bring another pet home. Inter-dog aggression, as it is called, is common amongst dogs. It happens when your dog is overly aggressive to a stray dog or an unfamiliar dog. Though this is quite normal, a dog can be unduly hostile because of several factors.

So what explains this kind of behavior?

- **Lack of proper training:** Prior to 14 weeks of age, your dog should be given a lesson on how to behave with other dogs. An easy way of doing this is to allow your dog to mingle with other dogs when he/she is smaller. Dogs love to play and sometimes, unconsciously, we can influence our dogs behavior in a big way. It is recommended that you be gentle with your dog and use toys to play with them instead of your body.

- **Past trauma:** If your dog has been traumatized in some manner in an earlier encounter with a stranger, he/she won't respond well to meeting a new dog. Here too, the owner's behavior might influence your dog. If at some point, you showed more compassion towards the timid dog and punished your own dog, he/she won't accept the dog the next time they see it.

- **Fear and anxiety:** Sometimes dogs fear losing their territory or social status. That sounds ridiculous, doesn't it? But it's true. One of the main reasons for aggression is fear and the thought that they might lose their holding.

How do we solve this?

There is no sure shot way to treat this. The only way you can diminish the problem is when you can control the situation. Introducing your dog to other dogs in a positive environment will go a long way in helping your dog realize that not everyone is a threat.

Punishing your dog when he shows aggression won't help in any way. When a dog is under severe duress, he/she will stop learning. It's a fight or flight situation for them at that point. Acute stress will only help him/her remember a traumatic incident connected to a dog and that can only increase aggression.
No matter how serious the problem is, improvements can always be made through both management and behavior modification.

In order to attain success, there must be committed to multiple lessons with a trainer.
There is no quick fix for aggressive behavior. Because many dogs exhibiting aggression have little to no formal training, several sessions may first be needed to teach necessary skills before the dog is prepared to encounter dogs or people.
The owner shouldn't confuse the dog with different tactics. Punishing him/her one day and reinforcement the next will confuse the dog further.
Successful treatment of inter-dog aggression is usually measured by the decrease in severity or frequency of incidents. In addition, the treatment recommendations need to be used over the entire lifetime of the dog. Even if aggressive incidents are completely eliminated for a period of time, relapses may occur if the owner does not strictly adhere to the rules at all times.

Don't wait for the dog to become full grown to start teaching him/her how to behave. To prevent a puppy from becoming aggressive, never let him/her play aggressively or play anything that shows them that they are dominant. Even if you do, make sure you win all the time and show them who's boss. It's important to make it clear to the dog that you own all the toys. You can also decide when and which ones the puppy can play with.

Playing is very important for dogs. This is their sure short way of exerting dominance over another dog, toy or even a person. Spaying or neutering your dog can help reduce some aggressive behavior or impulses to be aggressive. It can be difficult at times to differentiate between play or a violent encounter, but one of the best ways to stop it is to break up the fight before it starts. Understand your dog's body language so you can spot signs of aggression before it escalates. The most common signs of aggression are when they start to expose their teeth or adopt a low pitched growl.

A trauma stricken dog might behave in a completely different way, in which case don't punish your dog for showing aggression. Understand his/her symptoms and contact your vet for help.

A very small part of inter-dog aggression comes from genetics, too. But it's a very small part. Sometimes breeds such as Pit Bulls are bred to fight, in which case they are taught to be aggressive. Having said that, I personally think, a breed is never an indicator for predicting any kind of aggression. A friendly breed, like a Golden Retriever or a Labrador can be as aggressive as a Pitbull. And a Rottweiler can also be used as therapy dog. Their breed doesn't determine the reason for their aggression in anyway.

Are you thinking of bringing home a new pup, and are you worried that your older dogs will show aggression? Dogs normally don't show aggression towards a pup. But just to be sure that the pup won't get traumatized, it's better you introduce them in a neutral environment and supervised. Puppies are unusually brave and curious and will want to be around an older dog. Keep your older dog on a lease and make sure he/she doesn't lunge towards the pup. Signs like wagging tail should help you understand how your dog feels about the pup. Once they get friendly, it should be easier for you from there. A pup is most likely to learn from an older dog. Your older dog might take the pup under his/her wing and teach them a thing or two. Constant supervision is absolutely a must, even 5-month old puppies still need to be supervised. When you can't be there to supervise, exercise the puppy before crating him. He/she will naturally want to rest. But don't overdo it, crating a puppy all the time until it is big enough is absolutely the wrong thing to do. Crating doesn't create social skills and social skills are what are going to get them through. Always stay calm and assertive when speaking to your dogs.

Looking after a puppy

Bringing home a pup requires a lot of thinking. If you think you aren't ready for the responsibility of looking after a pup, then you should wait till the time is right. If you are a new pet parent, chances are you'll have sleepless nights, too. A pup ideally eats 5-6 times a day and during this period, constant monitoring is required. How, what and when to feed a pup are just a few things that you need to remember.

When you bring a pup home, it's ideal to find out he/she is being fed before. Maintaining the same nutritional theme is a good idea, at least for a few days, as a change in eating habits can upset the puppy's tummy. A puppy can be in stress about being separated from his/her mother, the rest of the litter, to his/her new home. A change in diet can increase the stress and upset the stomach.

How to help a pup adjust

Keeping the pup's food the same is one way to minimize the stress of the move. It is an easy way to bridge the gap that way. Always ask for a sample of what the pup has been eating. If you want to change the food in anyway, introduce the change gradually. Slowly introduce the new food and the old food together. Then wean him/her off the old food gradually. Continue for a few days and slowly the pup will be eating only the new food. This will help in a big way. It will minimize stress and prevent stomach upsets and diarrhea.

What do you need for a pup to adjust?

A pup needs all the right nutrients to grow rapidly. But what exactly to feed them? Should we give them milk, canned or dry food?
Firstly, whatever it is that is fed to the pup, you must ensure that it is complete, wholesome and balanced.
This may come as a surprise to you, but most animals are lactose intolerant. Puppies, with their delicate constituency,

can only stomach watered down milk, as a supplement to their mother's milk.

When it comes to solid food, the question is, what kind of food do we feed them. Canned or dry?

A combination of the two will do just fine. Dry food is less expensive, but the wet food agrees more with the little ones' stomach. Dry food can be a little more exciting by adding a spoonful of hot water on top of it to bring out the aromas and soften the texture.

Some new owners might want to feed their pup their choice of food and keep the food in the bowl all the time and the puppy simply grazes whenever it's hungry. This is not a good idea as some puppies may eat too much and become overweight. Plus, it may make housebreaking more difficult. If the "ad libitum" approach is to be employed, dry food is the way to go as it keeps better.

When does one feed a pup?

Pups that are around eight weeks old should probably be fed three or four times a day at first though the frequency can be lessened to three times a day by 12 weeks and to twice daily by 16 weeks of age. Feeding a pup in small quantities is a good practice as it permits the owner to make a note of the pup's eating habits.

At this stage in a puppy's life, the gastrocolic reflex is still quite active, so once a pup has finished eating, it usually has to be taken outside to eliminate. On doing this the pup will associate feeding with outside excursions, and this is a very good way to start the pup's training.

Where should I feed the pup?

It doesn't matter too much as to where, but it does matter how consistent the location is. To help the newcomer learn the ropes, feeding in the kitchen is usually a good idea as the pup will be near family members and kitchen floors are usually fairly easy to clean. There is nothing wrong with feeding a puppy in its crate or in a pen or in the living room.

How much should I feed the pup?

Now how do you know the right amount to feed a pup? It can't be too little, nor can it be a lot. But if you don't know the right amount, consult a vet. The manufacturer's instructions can also be your guide. There will be a range of quantity depending on your pup's size. Feed the middle of the range. If the pup woofs his food down within 2 or 3 minutes, his meal size may need to be increased. If there is still food left in the bowl after 15 or 20 minutes, the meal size should probably be reduced.

Puppies too have caloric requirements and they differ from one to the other, according to the pup's body weight. The ultimate gauge as to whether you're feeding too much or too little is the pup's size and condition.

Ensure that the pup eats during specific meal times, and doesn't "beg" for food when someone else eats. When meal feeding, especially if wet food is used, the food should be picked up after about 15 or 20 minutes so that none is left lying around. Always take your puppy out for a walk after the meal.

Should I feed my pup treats?
Healthy treats are the best and can be either part of the puppy's normal ration that is held back to be supplied periodically throughout the day for reward pleasing behaviors. Wet food is more of a reward than dry food. Treats should be small and should not be given often as they will imbalance the diet. Human food should not be given to pups, which they will obviously prefer. They can turn out to be finicky eaters and turn sickly. It's a bad idea to feed the pup from the table as this will develop into a bad habit. They will get into a habit of begging and pestering people during meals. You need to start out the way you intend to continue. A puppy will get confused if you aren't strict with them. Some people think it's okay to feed a puppy raw food. This is a strict no-no. Raw food, meat especially, can come with a lot of disease. It can wreak havoc with your pup's intestinal tract. The pup's intestine is really sensitive and it won't take long before the pup starts to vomit and then gets dehydrated and weakens in the process.

The vet might also advise you to give the puppy vitamin, calcium or mineral supplements at times. If at all there are any nutrients lacking in the pups diet, only then is it necessary to supplement their diet. If you have been feeding the pup a balanced meal, then these supplements are unnecessary.

The bottom line is that puppies should eat regularly and their eating habits should be observed to make sure that they don't eat too much or too little and that it does not become sick. Although this sounds pretty simple, plenty of us get it wrong and that leads to dire consequences.

Feeding pups at night.
Since a pup needs to eat at least 5-6 times a day, feeding a pup at night can give you sleepless nights. But don't worry; we have a few tricks for you.

Feed your puppy rather late and then allow at least one hour after eating before taking the pup outdoors to eliminate. The later you make the last feeding, the less chance your puppy will have a bowel movement during the night. You should give your puppy a chance to eliminate just before you go to bed. Make it a habit and the pup will get used to the routine. Crate the puppy, with a soft blanket and a stuffed animal or a chew toy. Don not keep any food or water around. As mentioned before, puppies tend to over eat. Leaving food and water over night might make them eliminate in the crate at night.

Make sure you take your pup out when he/she cries, and praise him/her for going, but bring it back indoors and place it back in the crate. Do not play with your puppy or it will want to wake you up just to play. They might whine for a bit, but will fall asleep eventually. As your pup grows older, he/she will develop better bladder control and will go about the whole night without eliminating.

Sometimes, extremely small pups won't wake up to eliminate at night. You can then move the crate to the bathroom or a utility area. Leave newspapers on the floor and leave the crate door open so that the puppy can go on the papers. This can also be done if you don't want to wake up every night to take the puppy outdoors to eliminate.

The first night away from the comfort of his/her mother can scare the puppy. Place the puppy in a box right next to your bed, so as to comfort the pup if needed. Just let the puppy sniff your hand. A familiar smell should help him/her settle down. Make sure the puppy learns to sleep away from you as soon as possible. The faster he/she learns to sleep away from you, the less chance to develop separation anxiety when the pup is older.

Another reason to move the pup out of the bedroom is if you have children. If your puppy sleeps in your room and your children don't, you are telling the puppy that he/she is more important than the kids because it's allowed to sleep with the "alpha adults", when the children are not. This can lead to problems when your puppy goes through "social maturity." You might have to deal with unwanted behavioral issues.

How to deal with separation anxiety in dogs

Most purebred dogs come with genetic disorders. Each breed has a different set of disorders, and most of them inherit these disorders from their parents. Dealing with this can be quite difficult for first time pet parents. Separation anxiety is the most common disorder you'll find in your dog. And sometimes is unknowingly encouraged by the owner.

In this chapter, we will talk about separation anxiety and how to deal with it.

Identifying separation anxiety
This problem mostly has the following symptoms: Excessive salivation, destroying items in the home, scratching at walls, doors and floors, barking, whining and attempting to escape from the crate, or room.

Causes for the anxiety
Sometimes separation anxiety can be hereditary. It can even arise from acute trauma or by first time pet parents who build this anxiety unknowingly. As a first time parent, if you make a big fuss about leaving your pup for a bit, it is going to lead to big trouble. Your dog will be conditioned to being stressed every time you leave.

To a dog, pet parents are a source of comfort, confidence and security. They think of you as their pack. If you are going to carry your pup around every time you step out, and leave him/her at home as they grow bigger, you are asking for trouble. A sudden change in their routine can also bring about anxiety.

How to deal with anxiety the right way
Let's start with the pups. The only way to train a pup is by disciplining them. Exercise them, play with them, tire them out and only then show them affection. There should be a balance between patience, obedience and confidence in the pup. Develop his/her confidence in your leadership. This

will help the pup be confident when left alone. He/she trusts you to come home. He/she looks at you for guidance and leadership.

Although a vet might prescribe drugs to calm the pup's senses a little, this will be a temporary fix for the underlying problem and that is not a real cure.

When a pup is separated from the litter, he/she will tend to cry. And as a worried parent, you invariably tend to pick up the pup and comfort him/her. Unfortunately, you are rewarding the pup for crying and hence providing a positive reinforcing for his behavior. The obvious outcome is the repeated usage of crying to grab your attention and demand for your affection. This won't work for you.

From the very beginning, we need to teach the pup to settle quietly for long periods of times. Reward the pup for being calm, patient and settling down quietly. Even when the pup is out or playing with you keep your interaction with him/her to a minimum. Avoid constantly trying to get his/her attention. He/she must learn to entertain himself/herself with toys.

Earlier in this book, we spoke about crating. Crating is very important for a pup. Teaching the pup to accept the crate can be tough, but it's a necessary measure. A pup should also be allowed to get familiar with the house and its surroundings, but under supervision. He/she must learn the limits and boundaries of his/her environment. He/she must also gain respect for this environment and the people in it. As long as you keep your methods consistent, the pup will learn and respond the way you appreciate.

Simulated anxiety vs Actual anxiety

There is true separation anxiety, and there is simulated separation anxiety, in which the dog behavior appears to be separation anxiety but it is, in fact, a learned behavior.

Simulated separation anxiety takes place when the dog lacks leadership and self-control.
Whereas, actual separation anxiety takes place when the dog experiences real stress in the absence of the owner.
The dog will know he/she will get attention if he/she behaves badly. Even asking them to stay quiet verbally is giving them some attention. They instantly feel rewarded as you are giving them attention. This is just misbehavior on the dog's part. They don't really stress too much while misbehaving.

Stimulated separation anxiety is fairly easy to overcome gradually. Consistent obedience training, lots of exercise and strong leadership on your part will keep the anxiety at bay.

Importance of obedience training

Separation anxiety can be sort out with the help of obedience training and discipline. You should let your dog know what is expected of him/her and let his/her good behavior become a habit.

Spend time training your dog, and this doesn't mean just once a week. Make it a habit to give him/ her some training time every day. Show your dog how you want him/her to behave around the house and respond to daily routines. You must teach your dog to be respectful and to have confidence.

Rehabilitation takes a great deal of patience and having your dog understand what is expected of him/her. You and your family should be accepted as leaders and not dictators. The dog should look up to you.

Let's look at an example. Dogs do some real cute things. If your dog nudges you or paws you, your first instinct is to pet them. If this becomes a habit, the dog would obviously think that he/she is in control and that they can tell you what to do. In situation when he/she can't carry it out, they become stressed.

One of the other reasons for anxiety, dogs tend to watch routine. They like to follow routines. Your dog can recognize a series of actions. Though we are creatures of habit, you will have to change our routines slightly to help your dog better.

Use a different door, put your coat and bag in different places. Make changes to create a different picture. If you are watching TV, or working on the computer, and your dog gets up every time you get up, simply get up and sit down again.

Your dog does not have to follow you everywhere. Yes, he can watch but he should be able to wait until you request his company. These little changes will help teach your dog to have the self-confidence he needs to handle being alone.

Separation anxiety can be overcome, you can turn some dogs around fairly quickly; with others it takes time, consistency and a lot of patience. Exercise, obedience, and lifestyle training, leadership, rules, boundaries, and limitations, are all necessary for a dog to achieve balance. Keep your behavior around them consistent and see great results.

Strategies to stop incessant barking

To state the obvious, your dog is going to bark whether you like it or not. Let me correct myself there – they should! A dog that doesn't bark at all is a lot more worrisome than one who does. Barking can serve as an alert mechanism and even protect you against intruders. What we're looking to tackle here is what can be seen as incessant barking.

You may not be able to follow why your dog barks as much as he does, and why it never seems to stop. More than anything else, this is usually because of exactly that – you don't know why! Getting to the root of the problem is critical when it comes to dealing with barking issues. Understanding that provides you with several options. Have a look at the list below and see if your dog matches any of these situations.

Why do dogs bark?

- **Fear** – It's just possible that your dog is scared of something. It could be an object that looks odd to them, or a person they see. Observe the patterns and see if your dog is actually barking at anything in particular.
- **Loneliness** – If your dog is left in the house for long periods without any company, this is expected behavior. You may be dealing with an unhappy dog and you need to work out a way for him to deal with the issue.
- **Marking territory** – Dogs, and many animals, can be territorial. You need to see if that's what is actually going on. He could be seeing someone as an intruder and is just marking his space. This often happens with other dogs in the mix.
- **General excitement** – Well, of course. This can happen when someone rings the doorbell or there's a new member in the house. Needless to say, this is good behavior unless you happen to find it excessive.

- **Anxiety issues** – This is a heightened aspect of loneliness and could result in depression. Professional help could be warranted if you notice strong mood symptoms. It could still be handled by avoiding the aspect of your dog not having company.

Before we get to the rest of this chapter, make sure you've discovered the root of the problem. Get help if you're unable to. You can still go ahead and try the different techniques listed, but truly understanding your dog has more benefits than just dealing with barking alone.

Techniques

- **Remove the item**

    If your dog is barking at an item, or maybe looking at another dog, get a distraction in place. Avoid the interaction with the other dog or remove the object. This isn't always possible of course, but do it when it is. If your dog is barking at a passerby outside, bring him in. Draw the curtains in your house.

- **"Quiet"**

    You may want to train your dog to quieten up. To do this, we have to go back to the obedience training methods. Incidentally, you have to first train him to bark on command! You could say "bark" or "speak" while holding a treat in front of him. Don't give him the treat till he barks. Once he does, give him the treat and shower him with praise.

    Once he learns to bark on command, command him to be "quiet" and repeat this a few times in a calm, firm manner. Give him another treat as soon as he quietens down. Repeat the process in a similar manner as discussed in the chapter related to obedience training.

You want to be able to use this technique when visitors or new people come over. If it doesn't work, use a distraction or a toy.

- **Play**

    Sometimes, your dog is just really excited and needs to play. Tire him out. Play a game of fetch, chase or whatever you'd like to do to keep him engaged. This is critical when your dog has been alone for a good few hours.

    You could play with your dog before you leave and for a while when you're back. That habit could ensure he is engaged and too tired to keep at it with the barking.

- **Ignore**

    This can work if you think your dog is barking to catch your attention. Let the barking continue and ignore it. If your dog stops barking, slowly go ahead and shower him with some love or give him a treat. Do this a few times and see if it works. You may have to change your technique if it doesn't.

There are some people who use 'bark collars', which release a sound or deliver a sensation to quieten your dog. Personally, I am no fan of these items of control. They don't address the underlying problem. Why is your dog barking in the first place? That's the problem to solve.

More than that, it's a clash of values as far as I'm concerned. Every so-called 'issue' is a way for you to build a positive relationship with your dog.

Whatever you do, avoid yelling at your dog when he continually barks. He may assume you're actually matching his tone and think of it as a game! You don't want that working against you. There is no difference between having a kid to take care of and a dog. The emotions are just as pure, and you owe it your dog to give him your best.

Spaying or neutering your dog

Many pet parents have this question at the back of their head. Some of us don't follow through with neutering dogs at a specific age because we think of it as brutal. But the big question is: Is neutering your dog absolutely necessary?

Many vets have a difference in opinion. There is a lot of research conducted that also contradicts everything that you read and see. No research is perfect and experiences can differ. There is no right answer to this question. Find a vet who will answer most of your queries and who you will trust no matter what. (More importantly your dog should be comfortable with this vet.)
And then base your decision on that.

Early neutering is a controversial topic. Some researchers say that neutering before 14 months of age will lead to cancer and joint problems. This isn't true. Joint problems and cancer are relatively common in large dogs. There is no study to prove that problems arise because of neutering. But there are several studies that prove that neutering dogs have a plus point.

Neutering a dog before he/she reaches 6 months is a good idea. Your dog is definitely going to be healthier and less obese. He/she will be less aggressive. Neutering helps with dealing with some of the nasty behavior some breed of dogs exhibit.

The choice is obviously in the pet parent's hands. With no proof of risk of cancer, but a very healthy chance of bad behavior or getting into a fight, your dog's life is in your hands. From personal experience, I can say that neutering a dog only helps him in the long run.

Spaying female dogs before 6 months is less controversial. Preventing the first heat nearly eliminates the risk of breast cancer which is much more common than bone cancer.

Spaying or neutering your dog is part of responsible canine care. Not only does it help with the overpopulation problem and saving lives of countless animals, it also has many benefits for the individual pup who has had the procedure done.

What are the benefits of spaying and neutering?

- **Your female pup will live longer.** Spaying can help your female dog live longer without facing many serious health problems. It can prevent uterine infections, breast cancer and many other diseases. Breast cancer for canines is particularly dangerous, resulting in death for about 50% of canine cases. The most effective way to provide this protection is to ensure your dog is spayed before her first heat.

- **The male pup will remain healthy.** Neutering a male dog helps with behavioral issues, testicular cancer and any other serious canine diseases. For the best chance of avoiding these diseases, one must complete the procedure at around 6 months of age.

- **You are helping the entire canine community.** Spaying or neutering now means, lesser deaths later. Euthanizing a dog is quite common and this can lead to lesser euthanizing. Lesser strays running around, the better. Strays are more likely to cause trouble, such as destroying property, causing car accidents, and even biting children and adults. Issues like these can negatively influence an entire community's opinion about dogs, even though it's only a few strays that cause the problem. It's impossible to round up all the strays and teach them how to behave. Spaying and neutering definitely helps there.

- **Your female pup will be better behaved and will not attract males.**

After six months of age, un-spayed females mature and go into heat. This lasts up to two or three weeks at a go, twice a year. This does vary from size and breed. During this time, a dog is going through hormonal changes. And that results in howling and even urinating inside the house which eventually attracts other male dogs.

- **Your male dog will behave better.**
  An unneutered male dog will display a number of behavioral problems in an effort to woo the female. Unneutered dogs can also display more aggressive behavior. They might also mark their territory around your house. The fluid they squirt while marking their territory can smell nasty and takes some time to come off yours walls and furniture.

Last but not the least...

- **It saves you a lot of money.**
  Although the surgery costs money, the cost of caring for a litter of puppies is a lot more. It will involve their food, medical and miscellaneous bills that will crop up. Look for a low cost or government veterinary hospital to handle the procedure. Many animal shelters also require spaying or neutering before they will release an animal, and the cost is built into the adoption fee.

If you haven't yet spayed your dog, there is no reason to wait - unless the dog is being used specifically for breeding purposes.

Grooming

A dog needs to be regularly groomed for many reasons. It plays an important part of responsible dog care. A dog can look after him/herself. It's important to attempt one task a day and not let it pile up till the end.

Here are some grooming tips that can be used on an everyday basis.

- Check for ticks and fleas every day. Eliminating them is essential as they can jump back onto the dog's body.

- Check if your dog needs to have his nails trimmed. This can be a tricky issue as the nail has a nerve embedded in it. This nerve is known as the pith. While trimming the dog's nails, you must pay close attention to what you are cutting. Accidentally cutting the nerve can be very painful for the dog and can lead to bleeding.

- Determine how many times your dog needs a bath. You can ideally bathe him/her once or twice a month. Depending on the dog's activities.

- Use a proper dog shampoo and not a human shampoo to bathe the dog.

- Rinse the dog well after shampooing as leaving the shampoo on can irritate the skin.

- Check the ears of the dog regularly. If you notice any foul odor or debris, clean it out carefully. The skin around the ear is very sensitive. Consult the vet if you can't seem to get rid of the smell.

- Some dogs love bath time and get all mouthy during it. Try giving a bath toy to divert his/her attention.

- Don't spray water directly into the nose, eyes or ears. This can cause serious discomfort to the dog. Instead, you can use a plastic cup to direct the water.

- Make sure the water used is lukewarm and not too cold or hot. The dog's skin is pretty sensitive.
- Use a low heat setting on the blow dryer.
A dryer can be an effective way to keep your dog from making everything in your house wet as he dries, but be careful not to burn your dog. You can also help keep it safe by not pointing it directly at your pup, but a little to the side instead.

Certain dogs have different needs. Especially dogs with lots of folds on their faces. They can be more prone to skin disorders. Ensure that the skin folds are all cleaned properly and there are no remnants of shampoo left behind. Rinse thoroughly and dry the face carefully. Consult a vet for more specifics on grooming for different breeds.

Pet boarding

How do I select a boarding home for my pet?

Unfortunately, some of us can't take our pets everywhere we want to go. Although we would love to have them with us all the time, it's simply impossible. So how would you go about looking after your furry friend while you are away?

Many of us don't like the idea of kennels. I would personally never leave my pets at a kennel. Finding a friend who would oblige to look after your pets for a bit will be great, but most of us don't have that option.

Home boarding is a marvelous option for owners who don't like leaving their pets in kennels. You can find one which suits your convenience and one that caters to your dog's needs. But dogs come in all shapes and sizes, so here is a guide to finding the perfect home boarding host.

For your puppy

Finding a host for your puppy could be a slightly difficult task. A puppy will need 24/7 supervision and the host should be willing to provide constant supervision. When choosing a boarding, ensure that the home is safe for exploring. Puppies are curious and tend to get into mischief. Ensure that your pup also likes the home and is comfortable with the host. A stay-at-home parent or a retired person, who has the energy to look after the pup is ideal. Be sure to check to see if the home is puppy proof.

For your adult dog

When looking for a host home for an adult dog ensure that the host has a yard so that the dog can roam around when he/she fancies it. A large dog will need a lot of activity and the host should know that. You can find hosts with specific breed experience, too. Smaller dogs might be easier to look after, but a large dog needs a lot more care.

Anxious dogs

Earlier in this book, we spoke about separation anxiety that the dogs face when away from their owners. Boarding a dog that suffers from this can be a slight challenge. It's important to choose a host who can understand this well.
Choose a host who is calm, confident and, and can earn your dog's trust. Don't forget to question them about their experience.

For a senior dog

Find a host who has experience with senior dogs and knows the importance of taking it slow and being patient. You must consider someone who doesn't have younger pet residents or children. The right home will be easy for older pups, with safe floors and ramps or single levels. The host should also notice signs of sickness, distress and exhaustion. They must also know how to inject medication if needed and to perform CPR.

What to look out for at a boarding place?

The general attitude of the staff and the level of cleanliness are important when deciding who to trust with your pet's care. A few other things to look for include:

- Staff that interact with animals and seem to enjoy their work.
- Being allowed their own toys and blankets can be comforting to some dogs.
- Sleeping and relaxed dogs, rather than dogs who look anxious, are pacing or continuously barking.
- Outdoor play areas where dogs can socialize.
- Elevated trampoline dog beds or similar (something easy to clean and off the ground).

- Multiple resting places for dogs (both inside and outside).

Dogs will often feel more comfortable if they have their own bed, blanket and perhaps a toy. Do check to see if this is okay and perhaps bring a couple of spares and label everything so it doesn't get lost if it needs to be washed.

If you are using a pet sitter, it is better to write down instruction for them. Leave some cash for emergency medical expenses. Many vets have procedures in place to take note of your wishes should something happen to your pet while you are away. You can let them know what your budget is and what level of treatment you consent to and you could perhaps also leave your credit card details on file should you be out of contact for long periods of time while on holiday.

Dog sitting

Finding the right sitter is very important. It has to be someone who you trust and more importantly, your dog trusts. Try and choose someone who can take care of your dog and calm him/her if he/she gets nervous or anxious when you are away. It won't be a good idea to leave a very active dog with an older person. Always remember to match the energies.

For many dogs staying at home will be less stressful. For older pets, who love the comfort of their own home, employing a pet sitter will be ideal. Uprooting them from their home, to be sent to a boarding can be very frightening and stressful for them. Dogs with separation anxiety might be better off staying at home.

For a sitter, though sitting for someone else's dog is fun, becoming accustomed to the habits and needs of an unfamiliar dog is challenging at first. Gaining the dog's trust is important for having a good dog sitting experience.

It's of utmost importance that you make sure you understand the needs of your dogs. Make sure this person can be trusted to understand the rules and boundaries set by you. They shouldn't create a problem for you by not maintaining your leadership.

You should ideally find someone who can stay at home and maintain the dog's usual routine. This means keeping their walk and feeding and sleeping schedule the same.
But if you leave your dog at a different location with a sitter, it's a good idea to get them familiar with the place, prior to the stay. Any concerns or separation anxiety is prevented. The dog will be a lot more relaxed and will not worry about you being away.
If you choose to board your dog, look into the place beforehand. Talking to people who have boarded their dog there before and research about the place. The smell, the

energy and the feel of the place matter. Check if the caretakers and owners are nice and calm. If they react angrily towards the dogs, then it's not the best idea to choose that place.

Just because you leave your dog at a boarding facility doesn't mean you have to follow all of their rules. If you have specific requests for your pet, then you can ask them to accommodate for your needs. When you change the environment, it's good to also change – and increase – the daily challenges, the physical and mental stimulation. This keeps the dog's mind and body more relaxed and less focused on their primary pack leader being away.

Know that if you leave the dog at a kennel for a long time, they are going to spend most of their time in the kennel. So when you pick up your dog, he/she is going to have a lot of pent up energy. Take him/her for the longest walk of his/her life when you pick him up!

A dog walker can help share the responsibilities of walking the dog if you find someone who can't maintain the routine for the dog. Ones who are comfortable walking more than three dogs at a time are probably going to be the best handlers, even if you just have one dog.

Tell your sitter about toxic household items and foods. There are many food items that are a complete no-no for a dog. Your vet can provide you with an exhaustive list.

If you look into all of the above, you have taken proper steps to ensure a pleasant experience for your dog while you are away. Even if you aren't with your canine companion, a calm-assertive attitude will help keep you stress-free!

Adopting dogs

There are so many homeless dogs all over the world. Some of them are found in shelters and they are so many more that are looking for a forever home. Often people are reluctant to adopt shelter dogs because of all kinds of notions. This chapter will help you abolish those notions.

Problems:
A lot of people think that dogs that are found in a shelter have a disorder or some kind of a problem. Dogs are abandoned for many reasons. The perception is that dogs end up in animal shelters because they were strays, they were seized in police raids, or they were aggressive. So, they will tend to run away, they will have emotional problems because of how they were treated, or they are just vicious.

This isn't true. Dogs end up in shelters because their owners give up on them most of the time. It has very little to do with the dog's behavior. The sad truth is that a lot of people give up their dogs because they can't afford them or simple because they stopped being "cute".

The only thing wrong is that the dog lives in a shelter and not with a loving family.

History:
Unless the pet parents inform the shelter about the dog, (happens in very rare cases) the shelter will not know about the history of the dog in anyway. Knowing the history is useful, but having no knowledge about it isn't a bad thing in anyway. Giving the dog a new home is what is important, so don't dwell on the past.

Diseases:
Dogs might tend to pick up diseases when kept in kennels. They are susceptible to diseases that other dogs carry because of their low immunity when abandoned. The shelter normally takes care of giving the vaccinations. Shelters also

makes sure that dogs are free of fleas and worms, and they provide spaying and neutering as part of the adoption process.

Breeds:
So what if the dog isn't a pure breed? Unless you want to use a dog as a show dog, there is no exact use for a pure breed. Mixed breed dogs are better choice. They are generally free of genetic disorders or diseases. Mixed breed dogs are also just much more interesting looking, since they don't follow the strict standards required for purebreds.

Age:
Adopting older dogs are usually frowned upon. The idea of having a pup is very attractive, but you've the job of raising it all the way to adulthood. People don't realize that a pup will stop being cute once he/she grows up. Some even abandon the dog after the dog grows up. If you don't want to take the trouble of training a pup, then an older dog is ideal for you. Most older dogs are well-behaved and are already trained. If they do have any behavioral issues, they will be much easier to fix at this point — assuming that they show up at all, which they may not if you do things the right way.

Don't discount senior dogs, which are those aged 7 years or more. Senior dogs can be ideal for lower-energy households, or in situations where you don't want to commit for ten or fifteen whole years, but still want a loving companion. Senior dogs are very smart and can help you also train a younger dog, if you decide to bring one in.

Having a dog can change your life. It's lovely how much love and compassion they all have, even after being abandoned. But giving them new life will benefit you and them.

Having a dog can be engaging and calming, too. The next time you want to get a dog, get to the nearest adoption center. Don't shop, adopt!

Fostering a dog

Giving a dog a home for some time is a nice thing to do. When you agree to foster, you agree to take a homeless dog into your home and give him or her love, care and attention, either for a predetermined period of time or until the dog is adopted. Being fostered is a wonderful opportunity for a dog to prepare for his forever home. He will have more one-on-one time with humans, and he can experience more of the world around him instead of being limited to the confines of a shelter. It can significantly increase his chances of fitting in with his next family.

The foster parents can also help the dog get adjusted with the new forever home. Fostering can do great things to the human as well as the dog. The dogs can help you appreciate the world around you. If you're stressed or anxious, it is a wonderful way to relieve your stress. They'll help you feel calm and composed. They bring in so much magic into the world.

While fostering a dog, it's important to know not to get too attached to the dog. Remember, you are preparing the dog to detach himself from you and live with another human. If not, it can be damaging to his relationship with his new family. He can move on, but it will just make it harder for him. He has been abandoned as it is. It will only make it harder for him to trust humans.
You might wonder why an adoption agency would need a home to foster a dog. It's simple.

- Sometimes a rescue group doesn't have a physical shelter and depends on foster homes to care for dogs until suitable homes are found.

- In some cases, a puppy might be too young to be adopted and needs a safe place to stay until he or she is old enough to go to a forever home.

- A dog might be recovering from surgery, illness or injury and needs a safe place to recuperate. Some dogs might show signs of distress such as pacing or hiding in the shelter.

- Sometimes dogs are rescued from pharmaceutical labs or testing labs. These dogs have never seen the light of day and may not know how to mingle with humans. They don't experience the simple joys of life either like, getting cuddled or petted. Living with humans will teach them how to socialize.

- A shelter might not have the space to accommodate so many dogs at once.

Preparing your home for a foster dog

Do you have pets at home? Will the foster pet and your pet get along? The first thing you will have to do is make sure your pet's vaccination is up to date. Foster pets might pick up diseases from being abandoned and not looked after. If you want to foster puppies or kittens, you may be exposing your own pets to upper respiratory infections and worms or parasites. Get your pet cleaned up and then take the foster to a vet, too. A vet can also recommend anything precautions that you need to follow. If the shelter is funded, then they might help you with managing the cost of the vaccinations and medication. But mostly you will be responsible for bearing their costs.

Looking after a foster dog

Make sure you know the history of your dog. To protect foster animals in a new environment and to safeguard your belongings, it is necessary to animal-proof your entire house. Never underestimate what a dog can do. Most of them are always up to mischief. Unless they are sick or scared, a dog won't sit around doing nothing. Dogs are curious creatures and they will want to explore every nook and cranny of the house. Which is why animal proofing the entire house is necessary. Make sure the place is devoid of nails, toxic material, plants and anything potentially dangerous. If you want your house to remain in one piece, put away all that you value.

**Precautions to take by room:
Kitchens/Bathrooms/Utility Rooms**

- Dogs are pretty good at prying anything open with their little paws, so ensure that all cabinets are locked properly.
- Keep medications, cleaners, chemicals and laundry supplies on high shelves or in childproofed cabinets. Make sure nothing is left around.
- Dogs love digging in the trash bin. Keep trashcans covered or inside a latched cabinet.
- Ensure that spaces behind the washing machine etc are off limits so that your foster pet can't get inside.
- The most important thing is to make sure your foster pet doesn't get into your dryer or washer. Always keep the doors closed.
- Keep everything edible off reach. There are many food items that don't agree with a dog's health.
- This may sound silly, but keep your toilet lids closed. A puppy can easily drown.

Living room space:

- If you have many lamps and wires, TV, phones etc., you might want to make sure that the cords of all these electronics are wrapped in PVC pipes as to prevent the dog from chewing it.
- Toys can also be hazardous if swallowed. So ensure your child puts them away.
- Remove things like strings, yarn etc.
- Make sure your houseplants are kept away. Some plants might be poisonous and need be kept away. If a plant is dangling overhead, remove it too, they might want to leap and bring it down.

- Needles, threads, sewing and art supplies need to be kept away.
- Secure aquariums and cages that house small animals, such as hamsters or fish, to keep them safe from curious paws.

If you have a garage or a basement, make sure that there are no chemicals or detergents lying around. A foster animal can be kept in a basement. Move toxics to a higher shelf and keep everything secure.

Precaution in bedrooms.

- If a dog is scared, the bedroom is the last place you should keep him/her in. If they get under the bed, it's going to be really hard to get out.
- Keep shoes and laundry safe. Dogs and their love for shoes is well-known.
- Cosmetics, lotions, sprays etc. should be kept off limits. Locking them up is the best option.

Here are a list of things that you should keep a check on.

- Closet and bedroom doors should be closed when not being used.
- Always keep the dryer doors and washer doors closed.
- Close cabinet doors.
- Make sure computer wires are wrapped up in PVC.
- Ensure no potted plant comes in the foster dog's way. They can be toxic if ingested.
- Sharp objects and toys should be stored away.

Having fostering dogs at home can be a nice experience, as long as you make sure these tips are followed. Carpets and other soft surfaces can harbor diseases easily. It is also difficult to clean up accidents on carpet, especially when they seep into the carpet pad. Bathrooms and other areas with tile, hardwood or other impermeable surfaces are ideal places to house your foster animals.

If you have a yard, fence it and let the dog enjoy the space. Check to see if there is a chance the dog can dig and escape from the fenced area. The foster dog should be under supervision at all times. Your pet can be slowly introduced to the foster dog. You should keep the foster dog on a leash when introducing him/her to their new surroundings.

Traveling with your pet

Leaving your pet at home is the worst. You will not be happy about leaving your darling at home, with a sitter or at the boarding. There is always the choice of taking your pet with you on a trip, but there are many things you have to consider. Here are a few tips to ensure a trouble free trip.

Schedule a vet visit: The first thing you have to do is schedule a vet visit. Ensure your dog is up-to-date for vaccinations, and ask if additional vaccinations are required for the trip since your dog may encounter different threats, at your destination or along the way. If your dog is ill, it's best not to travel. But if it's unavoidable, then make sure you keep a copy of the dog's medical record with you. In case your trip is delayed, ensure you have access to a vet around your destination or simply learn the necessary aid yourself.

Plan the route you want to take: The route you want to take should have a lot of rest stops. The dog will have to get off to eliminate for his/her happiness. Your dog will want to sniff around and take in the new environment. Plan a 15 minutes break every few hours.

Book pet friendly accommodation: A lot of places allow pets, but there are some which don't either. Always check if your hotel is pet friendly. If you are out camping, ensure the campsite allows pets. Always check before hand to see if the hotel is pet friendly.

Check the weather: This can help prepare for issues like rain, snow etc., which can slow your travel. You should also make sure to avoid natural disasters like hurricanes etc. In case of snow, make sure your dog is warm.

Pack your dog's belongings: Pack a few of your dog's items and it will help feed and look after him/her along the way.

This is a list of what you might need:

- Food and food bowl
- Water, water bottle
- Leash, toys for chewing and fetching
- Medications
- Protective clothing
- Dog-safe insect repellent and sunscreen
- Water googles
- Blanket and dog towel
- Brush and shampoo
- Flea comb and tick remover
- Poop bags

Car sickness: Like humans dogs can get car sick. Before you leave on your journey, find out if he/she suffers from car sickness. Make sure you stop every time he/she feels sick. Some doctors will even prescribe anti-nausea pills so that the dog can sleep through the journey. It's best to feed your dog a few hours before you get in the car. Before you head out, take a nice, long walk, so he/she's ready to rest and relax for the trip.

Update your dog's ID: If your dog is lost on your trip, you want to find him as quickly as possible. If the number on his tag is your home phone number, this could be very difficult. Take the time to make an ID just for the trip, listing not just your cell phone number. You should even include a friend's number just in case.

Try and keep your routine: It is possible to do everything exactly as you would at home, but try and remain consistent. Try and feed your dog at the same time, you feed him/her at home. You should increase walk time, so that he/she can be less anxious or excited about the trip.

You won't necessarily drive down every time you go out of town. Here is what you can do, if you take different mediums of travel.

Driving with your dog.

It's advisable to crate your dog while driving. Unless you have someone to solely look after the dog. If alone, there are chances your dog can distract you and you can land up with serious injuries. It also prevents your dog from becoming a projectile if you have to stop fast, also reducing the chance of injury for both of you. Don't feed your dog a lot before you leave. Don't feed him/her during your travel either. Wait until there's a break and you can give her a small snack, preferably high in protein. It's also good to spend a little time playing or walking during the break to get rid of some pent-up energy. And of course, don't leave your dog in a parked car, especially when it's warm outside. Even if you leave a window slightly open, the car can quickly turn into an oven, and your dog will get dehydrated.

Taking your dog on an airplane.

Each airline will have different set of pet rules. You might need a certificate stating that the dog is in good health. Make sure you check beforehand what details/certificates are needed. You don't want to be surprised at the airport. Your dog will definitely be traveling in a crate and it will probably make everyone's lives easier if you crate your dog before you enter the chaos of the airport.
Don't overfeed your dog or make him/her drink a lot of water. Make sure he/she has access to water and doesn't get dehydrated. If your dog isn't flying with you in the main cabin, don't have a big goodbye scene. You'll only upset your dog. If you're calm, he'll be calm.

Keeping your dog calm during travel

Make sure you take something that the dog relates to comfort. Taking his/her favorite toy, bone or stuffed animal will help your dog relax and make him/her comfortable.

For a little extra calm, try rubbing a little lavender oil between your hands and give your pet a little aromatherapy massage.

Sedating a dog

Although I don't recommend this, a dog can be given prescribed pills only if he/she is extremely scared or anxious when travelling. You might get stuck in the loop of giving your dog pills and he/she might start to rely on them completely. This can have disastrous effects. Have faith in yourself, you can keep your dog calm with your attitude, voice and body language.

Go on a long walk once you reach the hotel

If you walk your dog enough, he/she will be more relaxed during a long trip. It's natural for a dog to be a little wary of new people or strangers. If you find them growling, doesn't mean he/she is aggressive. It only means that he/she needs reassurance. Show your dog that you are under control and he/she will relax, too. If a dog growls at someone don't pull him/her away from the person. Instead speak to him/her in a calm, reassuring tone.
Again, be calm and assertive and show your dog that you've got him/her covered.

Exploring a new place

Your dog is away from home and that means a lot of new sights, smells, sounds, and potential food items for your dog. Make sure you're checking on him/her throughout. Check what is around always, wherever you go about, especially in the area of things your dogs could ingest. Also, especially around the holidays, there may be a lot of lights, decorations, and snout-level treats that can be distracting or dangerous for your dog. Keep an eye on him/her in the new place.

How to enter the hotel room with your dog

As you enter your hotel room, don't let your dog stray away. He/she will think he/she is in control of the situation. Enter first. Get the dog to stay where he is. While you are unpacking, showering, or making phone calls, he is waiting. The only one who should move in the environment is you—until you are ready, then you initiate activity. It's important that your scent is everywhere before the dog settles in.

Traveling with a dog can be a fun experience for both of you. Just remember to be as prepared as possible wherever you go. The more homework you do on dog travel, the fewer surprises there will be. Don't forget to make sure your dog gets plenty of exercise and above all, of course, be calm and assertive. A balanced dog makes the best travel companion. So ensure his/her safety and you will happy a lovely trip.

Crating your dog for travel

It's natural to feel bad about crating your dog. After all, you wouldn't want to be crated. But don't project your feelings onto your dog. They don't mind the crate and some even feel safer in one. So don't make a fuss about it yourself. As stated before, you are the pack leader, he/she will follow your lead. If you panic, he/she panics too.

The most important thing you can do is make sure your dog has been well exercised before he/she goes in the crate. If he/she's burned off his/her excess energy, he/she'll be more inclined to rest.
Keep positive. Don't present the crate as a punishment or prison. The dog will hate it. Show the dog the crate and open the door. Don't shove the dog in the crate. Let him get in on his own. When he's inside and comfortable, you can close the door. Walk away with good energy and body language. If you make a sad voice, he/she will get anxious and start to bark or cause trouble. Come back in 15 minutes. This will ease the dog's separation anxiety next time you crate him/her. But don't take him/her out of the crate. Remember that you're not projecting that the crate is a bad thing. Just open the door and he/she can come out when he/she's ready.

Having a dog is a wonderful experience. Be it a puppy or an adult dog that was abandoned at a shelter, a dog's behavior will never change to come one who shows him/her unconditional love and respect. There is so much to learn and discover when it comes to a dog. They come with different kinds of emotions and a lot of taking care off.

Unfortunately, in today's world, a breed dog is seen as a trophy. He/she is misused to either breed more puppies or take part in competitions so that humans can have their interests taken care off. Try and spread awareness when it comes to pets. Stop mistreating them, explore all possible and means of obedience training and let man's best friend be your best companion. Hopefully these chapters will help you understand the world of dogs.

Dogs that eat their own...

I started writing that title and I wasn't sure I wanted to complete it. If you're new to the world of pups and dogs, prepare yourself for a possibility – your dog may decide to eat his own poop. That's right. It may not happen all the time if you're lucky, but it's common enough for us to look at. This tendency in dogs is termed as *Dog Coprophagia*. Doesn't that just sound better than 'poop-eating dog'?

While many dogs tend to outgrow this, we don't really want them eating their own feces! Thankfully, there are simple, proven ways to train them out of this. It's for these scenarios you should ensure that your dogs are vaccinated on time so they avoid dealing with any illness. First, let's understand why they do this.

Causes of dog coprophagia

- If your dog is not getting sufficient nutrients, he may turn to eating his own feces. It's important to ensure that you provide high-quality food to your pets at the right time. If the food goes undigested, dogs tend to look for other sources for their nutrients.
- Your dog may just be hungry if you're not feeding him on time.
- Your dog might actually like it! This sounds nasty, but it's possible and that's fine. You can deal with it.
- He may just be 'cleaning up' by getting rid of the poop from a particular area.
- It could develop because of certain medications, or your dog has a medical condition. If you feel that's the case and the techniques don't work as planned, take him to a vet.

How to get your dog to stop

- Ensure that you feed them good meals. This is important. Buy high-quality products and stick to the recommended timings.
- Exercise! It's been the answer to the human problem and it's the same with dogs. Keep them engaged and active. This helps their mood and their digestion.
- Clean any area with feces. You don't want feces lying around for your dog to find. Besides, picking up after your dog is just the right thing to do.
- Distract your dog with a toy or any other item.
- Try the "No" or "Leave it" command here. If that stops your dog from eating poop, reward the behavior immediately.

As usual, maintain consistency through all this. You'll be able to break that unpleasant habit in no time. It's important to keep a watchful eye over your dog so can apply these techniques, as with all other things.

Closing thoughts

I do hope that this book was helpful. I've tried to keep it as simple and concise as possible keeping the first time dog owner in mind. More importantly, this book was a design in step-by-step instructions that are easy to follow. In fact, I've imagined this to be a conversation with you to help you through it.

If you read this book and had your dog work with the instructions side-by-side, I'm sure you've seen the results. If you read this book in one go and you're set to get started, I wish you the best. I promise you that you'll enjoy the process as long as you have the patience. Be sure to have fun with it. This is all part of the experience of having a pet.

As you experience success in the process of dog training, I'm sure you'll learn to naturally communicate with your dog in your own style. The entire process in itself can build positivity and really help you understand your dog in a much better way. That's the hidden benefit of not hiring a trainer. The best person to work with your dog is you!

If you notice any specific problems, however, do not hesitate to take help from an expert. While most dogs respond to what we've covered, you may always notice some discrepancies. If you do, check if it's a medical issue or a trait that you may simply need assistance with.

If you liked what you read, do leave me a review on Amazon. I'd love to hear what you think.

With that, I shall bid you adieu and wish you a truly fulfilling relationship with your dog. You truly do have a best friend in tow. Good luck!

Bonus Chapter: Get some love!

So far, you've learnt all the essential things you need to know. We've looked at all of it in a positive manner. Now that you're nearing the end of this book, let's reward *you* now! We're going to look at two fun tricks for you to work with, and we're sure you'll enjoy it.

Get a kiss!

Lure your dog into kissing your cheek! Here's how you do it:

a. *Place a treat or something that they enjoy on your cheek. Some cream or any treat that can be placed on your cheek works.*
b. *Lean towards your dog. You know what he's going to do. Just as he's doing that, state your command - "Give kiss!"*
c. *Repeat the process a few times just as we have with all other trainings*
d. *Test it without the treat and there you go! You have yourself a kiss-happy dog.*

Paw shake

Well, this is the fun trick that everyone is interested in. It's almost a bit of a party trick when people come over. Your dog shouldn't really be about show, but why not have a few fun things happen too? When you take your dog for a walk, it could be another attention-grabber and a sign of safety to those interested in petting him. Dogs love attention, after all.

a. You'd definitely want him seated to start with. So get him to sit. Test your command!
b. Once he's seated, simply say "Shake" with his name as you lift his paw.
c. Let the paw go and do this a few more times with the command.

d. Eventually, you simply want to have your hand outstretched with the command and see if he responds.
e. If he does respond, go ahead with that resounding yes and give him a treat if needed.
f. Test this at different times, with breaks. Do this at different places. Don't keep going at it, you don't want to tire him out.

Test this with different people too. If you have other members of the family with you, use the same command and train him to respond. Accordingly, your dog will understand that this is a general gesture.

Please accept my sincere thanks for picking up this book. I truly hope that you have benefitted from it. If you liked what you read, I'd be grateful if you can leave a review by using the link below.

http://amzn.to/1XxMvHd

Printed in Great Britain
by Amazon